The UFO Thɛ

The Truth About Who Christ Was

Adrienne Jaffery

Adrienne Jaffery

Published by
TheOuterWorld Books

London, United Kingdom

..

Chapter Listing:

Introduction...1

PART ONE
Lost Secret: Jesus the Extraterrestrial

1. Speculation..**7**
2. Making the Claim.................................**17**
3. The Gospels.......................................**31**
4. Gnostic Gospel Proof............................**55**
5. Implications..**69**

PART TWO
The Ascension

6. Myth vs Reality..................................**75**
7. Analysing Luke and John.....................**87**
8. Da Vinci and Other Painters................**103**
9. Conclusion.......................................**121**

- -

The UFO That Took Jesus
The Truth about Who Christ Was

· ·

Introduction

This is certainly not the first time that I write about Jesus in the context of him being an extraterrestrial. In my previous book on the subject - appropriately titled **Jesus the Extraterrestrial**, I talked about scriptural evidence that points to a different interpretation and truth about Christ than what the Church Fathers and the Christian religion on the whole has always held firm to.

In that book, my primary goal was to give an overall image of how Jesus may be considered to have been an alien, especially in light of Gnostic writings, the Noble Qur'an and other religions both ancient and modern. The reception was mixed and it was never my aim to offend any Christians or other adherents to religions that believe in Jesus as a Holy Prophet. I was simply putting forward a proposition which if true, could be revolutionary for how we consider the ancient past, Christianity, the identity of God and so on.

This book is not only a continuation of that work but actually a re-writing of it. As such, I have split this book into two halves. The first half is the new version of my previous book 'Lost Secret' and the second half (page 75) elaborates on those ideas to focus more on the Ascension of Christ and the UFO that took him. While it is a continuation of sorts, it proposes a theory. I talked for no more than a couple of paragraphs in my last book about this monumental event in the gospel story and in Christian theology but this book is centred around the notion that Jesus of Nazareth was an extraterrestrial being who left earth on a spacecraft to go back to the place whence he came.

If you're new to Ufology or Ancient Astronaut Theory, you may be skeptical and maybe you even think I'm a delusional person, or crazy! However, I won't be the first person to believe in extraterrestrial involvement in humanity's history and evolution and I won't be the last. Claude Rael, Eric Von Daniken and other UFO believers have discussed in depth how somewhere in our evolutionary line and distant past aliens interacted with us. I am however one of the first people to discuss in depth how Jesus fits into the story of mankind with concerns to extraterrestrials and UFOs. Before you judge my assumptions and say I'm just another conspiracy theorist, I'll say with modesty that I am not clueless about the Bible and Christianity. In fact, I hold a degree in Theology & Religion as well as a Master's degree. That by no means signifies I'm some kind of expert but I do know a thing or two about the New Testament as this is my particular area of interest.

If you choose to take this book as an offensive gesture towards your beliefs, I will say that you're entitled to that opinion and I am sorry, but I will urge you to read the whole book and to hear me out. If you decide that I am a loon, that's okay too. Aren't we all, to some degree? Jokes aside, take everything with a pinch of salt. Of course most of what's in this book is speculation that is well-backed by scripture but I am not going to be making radically ridiculous claims either. You can come to your own conclusions and I won't be shoving any of my personal beliefs down your throat. The aim is to present a bunch of evidence which I think is intriguing and thought-provoking. You can do with that what you will. More than anything else though, I really hope you enjoy my book and to this end, I want to thank you for choosing to purchase it. If you like it and find it interesting, I kindly ask that you leave a review afterwards as this helps me out greatly.

Thank you as always,

Adrienne Jaffery

PART 1

LOST SECRET:

JESUS THE EXTRATERRESTRIAL

1

When one reads a claim so bold as 'Jesus of Nazareth was an extraterrestrial', extreme skepticism follows. It's even worse when you take the risk as an author to dedicate an entire book to defending such as assertion. In order to convince anyone, you need evidence and a lot of it, you need facts and more than anything, you need to be convincing.

I was aware of all of these factors when I first decided to write a book on the subject and it took me many years to put pen to paper, so to speak. I deem it absolutely pivotal to introduce the subject and its history before delving into the meat of the claim. That is, why even write on the topic? What significance does it have and what sort of claims have been made in the past?

The risks I take when writing this book without an anonymous name are dire yet I have held the views that I will share in this text for many years. It is my truth based on everything that I have researched inside of and on the outskirts of the fields of theosophy, ufology, sacred sexual spirituality, and of course, biblical studies.

In this project, I am not taking a rigorous or strict academic approach. Since the subject at hand is so close to my heart, I will simply present arguments and points of significance from which you might make your own determinations.

Numerous readers will consider the arguments in this work controversial and maybe even crazy. Moreover, I am fully aware of the potential blasphemy and offence that might be taken from conservative Christian circles and for that, I apologise.

Moving on now from the disclaimer, let us explore the world of alternative mysticism and more importantly, the history of the claim that Jesus, son of Mary was indeed other-worldly. Jesus of Nazareth is without a doubt the most spoken about figure in the world of Religion and maybe the most known human being who ever lived. Yet, almost nothing   factual is known about him. Even the question of whether he existed or not remains a point of debate in some academic spheres.

Other than in the four canonical gospels of the New Testament, the gnostic texts of the Nag Hammadi library and the writings of St. Paul, no accurate source for Jesus' life can be found. Even these sources are convoluted and tainted by the writers' own socio-political and religious agendas.

It is mind-boggling that so much attention has been given to a man who we don't even know anything about with certainty. So much speculation exists around Jesus that any form of document or scroll put forward claiming something immediately becomes a focal point for the media. This was especially true in somewhat recent times on two occasions. Firstly, with the 1947 discovery of one of the original seven Dead Sea Scrolls: the Pesher Habakkuk which archaeologists label as 1QpHab.

The scroll is an early commentary from a Qumran writer on the prophetic (Nev'im) book of Habakkuk from the Old Testament. There is mention of a Teacher of Righteousness and a Wicked Priest. What is known now is that the document is unlikely to have been alluding to Jesus, but at the time, countless radio interviews and scholarly debates occurred.

The second occasion where speculation about Jesus caught the world's attention was in Dan Brown's novel and later adapted motion picture (2003), The Da Vinci Code. The main claim of the film, regardless of the plot, is that Leonardo Da Vinci deliberately painted John the apostle (who is sat next to Jesus in the Last Supper) as effeminate because he was discretely suggesting that it was actually Mary Magdalene sat next to Jesus.

The way they are positioned in the painting creates a V shape between them which is suggestive of sexuality i.e. that Jesus and Mary Magdalene were intimate.

As well as in popular culture, so much has been written about Jesus in academic fields. Not only in the obvious disciplines such as theology, Biblical studies, religious studies and the philosophy of religion but also in gender studies, sexuality studies, animal studies, ecology and many more.

Topics which have arisen by numerous academic writers include: whether Jesus was a woman, whether Jesus was intersex (former outdated and politically incorrect term: hermaphrodite), whether Jesus was an environmentalist and so on and so forth.

To add to this increasing list of how Jesus has featured in numerous aspects of the human world, even in the imagination, he is focal. For example, the expression 'Jesus Christ!' is used commonly in the English speaking world for many scenarios. It is utilised when expressing fear, shock, anger, amazement, awe, disappointment and I'm sure for various other emotions as well as those just noted. More importantly, it's used without second thought.

You could be at a soccer (football) match and your team has just conceded a goal. A fan will express 'oh Jesus Christ!'

Alternatively, you might be at a grocery store and someone drops an item of food, 'ah Jesus Christ!' Again, you could be at a party drinking alcohol in excess and the next day, someone asks you how much you had to drink. When you tell them, they answer with 'Jesus Christ!'

We have all heard someone say it at least once a day since we were born. Isn't it fascinating that even though we use that expression, it seldom has anything to do with Jesus himself. When you consider this properly from the outside, you begin to realise how uncanny it is.

Jesus Christ, his name, what he did, how he lived and died has an influential staple in almost everything we do in the western world. Foods (hot cross buns for instance), many flags of the world (England, Wales, Great Britain generally, Scotland, Northern Ireland to name a few), Christmas (even though Jesus was not actually born on the 25th of December) and so on.

Jesus Christ has influenced the world in every single way imaginable and yet, we know nothing factual about him. That is what we are dealing with whenever discussing any attribute of his being.

So as one might imagine, speculation that he was an extraterrestrial, let alone a woman, an intersex person or anything terrestrially tangible seems beyond far-fetched.

Yet again, another problematic element of any conjecture concerning Jesus is the way in which the world perceives him today. We are two millennia past the supposed time that he walked the earth. The cultural, political and religious affiliations surrounding Jesus render it laborious, if not impossible to convince anybody one way or another. For skeptics, Jesus being a creature or a person from a different world seems logical upon reflection of comparative religion and the Bible.

However, for the majority, it is a ludicrous postulation. Writers who dare make the move to content which is original and innovative regardless of truth are shamed as being delusional and in the words of a critic I met "nutty and mental."

All is well though. Not everybody can be convinced. The sole thing I ask for in my reader is an open mind and the ability to question and reflect. It has always been my estimation that a well guessed approximation based on evidence is better than never knowing at all.

On that note, all that I can assert is that I am tackling the topic in this book to the best of my ability and I hope that you consider my attempt a decent one. As times change and as Biblical studies fades out in its contemporary relevance, something other needs to take its place. We cannot just set the Bible and apocryphal literature aside and discard it as something of the past when we haven't even begun to enquire into the complexities of the issues that remain unknown.

With the rise of a secular millennial generation who care not about religion or ancient history (at least for the most part), something needs to replace the hole that is left when the fields of Theology and Biblical studies eventually come to a halt.

Study into the historical Jesus and ancient Israel need a solid reset. Alternative theories are needed at this point in history. The scientific method and archaeology have failed to scratch beneath the surface and provide us with an accurate portrait of who Jesus might have been. I, as well as other conspiracy theorists are not satisfied with the plain view put forward by the likes of Reza Aslan: that Jesus was a trouble maker. A rebel from Galilee who considered himself a prophet with controversial political views.

There is something more to the authority and personhood of Jesus. To say anything else is negating the influence he had on history and further neglecting the fact that some early groups of his followers clearly saw a light in him which cannot be reflected through mere history books or religion.

2

Every claim about Jesus' authority and personhood that I was force fed never felt right in my heart of hearts. I loved Jesus, I saw him as a missionary and the greatest being to ever have walked the earth. I believed in his message, his parables, his miracles but there was always that one thing. The thing that no matter how much I wanted to believe as veritable never absorbed in my mind as true: who he was. From a very early stage in my theological education, I realised that the Jesus of the gospels was not the Christ of faith. There is such a disparity between the two.

If you observe and study the history of Christianity, so much reformation occurred since Jesus' death that the Christian religion became something so different to what Jesus himself would have wanted.

It seems so evident that the preacher of Galilee would not have wanted structure in his message, he probably wouldn't have even wanted a religion based upon him altogether. Controversially, I would posit that Christianity is an insult to Jesus, whether extraterrestrial, human or whatever else.

Every story, parable, metaphor, ethic and action of Jesus in the New Testament has been interpreted beyond any need and transformed into an absolutist misconstruction. The Jesus that I have always loved would never have wanted what we call Christianity. That is why books such as this one are needed. Books and theories which consider Jesus as himself: a man with a message riddled with mystery that need not have anything to do with 'God' himself.

When I was at the peak of my Christian journey, near the time that I was baptised, I would spend hours performing lectio divina: the practice of reflecting through prayer on Biblical passages.

Each and every time that I fell upon the sermons of Jesus, particularly in Matthew 5-7 and 13, despite my convictions about God, I could never trust the Christian interpretations. It always appeared to me that Jesus was concealing a great truth about his nature. He was not telling the whole story and even those explicit references made about his Father did not sound like an omnipotent God.

That is one of the main reasons I abandoned the Church. I desired so greatly to seek truth, no matter how far-fetched it might be. So often would I feel like a traitor, ashamed to vocalise what I thought about Jesus. I still adore Jesus and what he stood for, I just cannot conceptualise him as the son of a deity.

I am less apologetic for my views these days. Certainly, I am considered wild for my beliefs about who the man might have been but in my mind, the belief in God, especially YHWH (the God of the Bible) is lunacy. We have all the appropriate sources from the Ancient Near East that suggest that the Judaeo-Christian deity (once deities) is a reformulated version of the Gods of Canaan before the twelve tribes apparently settled. He is not and was never one single identity. Even across the Bible, God takes on different attributions and personalities.

He is sometimes jealous (Exod 20:5), other times he is gracious (Ps 86:15). Once more, at other points he is angry and vengeful (Deut 6:15). The faces of God in the Christian canon (Old and New Testaments) are inconsistent at best. Even the names of God change throughout and there is no apparent logical narrative flow. An even greater contrast is found in the New Testament. Novel ideas arise seemingly out of nowhere which indeed can confuse any reader who reads the Bible chronologically.

All of a sudden between the book of Malachi and the first gospel (Matthew), the idea of heaven presents itself, God is a far more forgiving entity who has provided mankind with his son as a sacrifice, and most importantly, Jesus comes to essentially embody the Torah and initiate the commencement of a new era. All of the laws in the Old Testament are made void so long as one believes in Jesus.

At least with the extraterrestrial theory, it is a concrete possibility which isn't based on any supernatural or theological outlook.

I am calling for all readers of this book to open their minds and detach themselves from what they think they know. That is, Jesus being the founder of Christianity and the son of God. I would initially like to consider two men who made the claim before my time.

Since the 1970s, two prominent figures have led movements which made the claim famous around the world: Jean Sendy, Claude Rael and Erich von Däniken. I will begin with the former: a man called Claude Vorilhon, who now goes by just Rael which means 'messenger of God'.

I will admit that Sendy is the man who first got me intrigued by the whole idea of Jesus being an alien but Rael's account is pretty bizarre. His story starts in 1973. Vorilhon was a race-car enthusiast and journalist in Clermont-Ferrand, France. He had his own car magazine and was a defined atheist.

. .

On the 13th December 1973, when he was taking a stroll in the volcanic region of the countryside of Puy de Lassolas, he saw a shining object in the sky approaching. As it lowered, he noticed that it looked like a large bell and was completely metallic all around.

The craft landed and he approached carefully. An opening at the base of the vehicle made itself manifest and out came a small human-like being who greeted Claude.

Rael claims that the being told him that its name was Yahweh (the name that was revealed to Moses as the name of God). Yahweh is one member of the species that is 25,000 years more scientifically advanced than us and created mankind using DNA manipulation when they discovered a smaller planet than their own. Rael further claims that this species, called the Elohim (another name for God in the Bible - particularly in the book of Genesis) made early Israelites and humans across the ancient world believe they were gods because they were not intelligent enough to comprehend the truth that these creatures in reality, were extraterrestrials.

In his own words, Rael states that the idea of God in the Bible, Qur'an and other religious texts actually is a metaphor for these beings who helped with our evolution and societal formation.

The Raelian religion/movement formed shortly after and according to Claude, the Elohim have been in contact with him ever since. He believes himself to be the last Messiah and messenger to mankind. Rael considers himself to be part of the same messianic and prophetic family as Ezekiel, Muhammed (صلى الله عليه وسلم), Jesus, Abraham and Noah.

His writings are mainly the messages given to him by Elohim to transmit to the rest of mankind. Adherents of the religion believe in free-love, polygamy, eternal happiness and freedom from belief in a non-existent God.

Their ultimate hope is to build an embassy (which several nations have agreed to host) which will be used as a landing pad for the Elohim before 2025 (this date is correct as of the movement's declaration in October 2017).

Regardless of whether Rael is to be believed or not, the theory is interesting in and of itself and when considered with a pinch of salt, it makes one wonder of the 'what if'. So where does Jesus feature in the peculiar world of Raelism?

In Rael's book 'Le Livre Qui Dit La Vérité' (The Book Which Tells The Truth), he talks an awful lot about Jesus' role on earth and in the mission of humanity. He puts forward a narrative that Yahweh impregnated a young Nazarene girl (Mary, the Virgin Mother) in her sleep so that Jesus would be born as a hybrid of the human-elohim variety. The reason the species Elohim wanted to create a hybrid was two-fold.

In the first instance, they were curious to see what conflicts a human hybrid would have. Humans are carnal and put great emphasis on animalistic desires whereas according to Raelian literature, Elohim are far more sapio-centric and put heavier onus on the value of unconditional love. The experiment that was Jesus, if Rael's claim is to bear any degree of credibility, was more about testing the similarities and differences in Elohim and humans so that they might ultimately reveal themselves to humankind.

The second reason is that the Elohim wanted to reveal themselves in a subtle manner, appropriate for the first century. This relates back to the point made by Rael in his book that the Elohim have wanted to reveal the truth of who humans are and who their creators are, for a long time.

To expand on this, if the Elohim landed on earth in Judaea during the Roman Empire, the Jewish population of that time would have claimed that the act was caused by God or some act of divine intervention.

This contradicted the aim of the Elohim which was to be upfront and honest about the nature of their existence. So, they decided to reveal themselves through an actual person who had Elohim in him. The miracles of Jesus in this theory were an act of demonstrating who he really was: a scientifically advanced being who was half human and half creator (Elohim).

If the Raelians are correct, even though the Elohim tried to announce their truth in a lighter manner than presenting themselves in spacecrafts, they failed nonetheless.

This is because Jesus was still perceived as God and as the son of God despite his attempts to teach small groups of Jewish adherents that 'if you really know me, you know my father as well' (Jn 14:7).

I have studied the Raelian movement for four years and despite some interesting theories and postulations, I discredit the basis of their religion entirely. I do not believe Rael's story or authority and furthermore, based on the testimonies of ex-members and constant lies which can be disproved time and time again, it all seems like an ego-centric attempt to control people in a cultic fashion. Rael being both culpable and responsible, first and foremost.

Nonetheless, one aspect of the story which in my opinion bears some level of merit, is the aforementioned view about Jesus and who he was. After I stopped studying the Raelians and resumed a normal academic life, I could not read the gospels in the same manner again.

As I will demonstrate in the next chapter, when we strip Jesus away from the Christian setting that theologians across the centuries have placed him in, we can begin to navigate his words and actions in the gospels in a new way.

Before diving into scriptural evidence, the second influential figure who made the claim famous ought to be discussed. Erich Von Däniken shocked the world in 1969 with his best seller 'Chariots of the Gods?' which made the claim that the deities in every religious book from history depicts the work of an ancient extraterrestrial civilisation and not the work of divine beings.

Similar to Rael, Däniken believed that early humanity was not advanced enough to comprehend who these beings were. Therefore, the humans of the bronze age wrote in their respective literature that unexplainable works were performed by God or 'the Gods'. Unique to Däniken's view is the idea that across the centuries, the civilisation that was involved in early human development sent enlightened beings to earth. These beings which he called the 'sons of God' would teach mankind of spirituality, mathematics, philosophy and tools which render humans unique among other animals. Jesus was one of many of these 'sons of God'.

There is not much else that needs to be said about Von Däniken's work since he only ever references Jesus specifically twice across his entire bibliography. Nonetheless, the setting of his beliefs about the origins of humanity is indispensable when going in depth about Jesus being potentially from another world.

In this chapter, I have considered two key writers in making the claim about the nature of Jesus. In reality, one could mention dozens of writers and artists who have had the same thought on the issue however, that would not advance the research on the topic further.

Now, we have a basic setting for the assertion (that needs to be at the forefront of the mind when going further) i.e that Jesus was sent by extraterrestrials for a purpose. What ought to now be investigated is the hard evidence which suggests that Jesus was someone or something much more than just the son of the Judaic God.

3

The aim of this chapter is to demonstrate how the gospels might be reinterpreted for a contemporary audience, with focus on the verses which are striking, both in an uncanny way and in ways which do not make apparent sense upon first glance.

For the sake of simplicity, I will not recall each gospel in order, since this would be a pointless exercise which would not be accomplishable in one measly book. Exegetical commentaries on individual gospels can be as long as five hundred pages long and doing this sort of analysis would defeat the purpose of this work. Instead, I will draw upon individual verses and try to reconstruct the most important aspects of Jesus' teachings and life.

Please note, for the sake of abbreviation that I might use the term 'synoptic gospels'. This refers to the first three gospels which are often grouped together in New Testament Studies. This is because in the popular academic model of authorship, the   four source hypothesis, it is generally agreed that all three authors used a lost source (Q) as the foundation for the constructed narrative found in these three gospels. This explains why all three share so much similar content. It is further thought that Mark was used by Matthew and Luke might have been aware of Matthew.

For example, eighty per cent of the content of Mark's gospel (the earliest written gospel) is found in Matthew and over sixty percent of Luke is also found in Matthew and so on.

Baptism

We begin with how Jesus began his mission among earthly men. The baptism of Jesus has been depicted in countless paintings in Western art. But very few have actually read the accounts of the baptism in the gospels. This narrative is recalled in all four gospels. I will cite Matthew's account which for reference sake is paralleled in Mk 1:9-11, Lk 3:21-22 and Jn 1:29-34.

"As soon as Jesus was baptised, he went up out of the water. At that moment heaven was opened, and he saw the Spirit of God descending like a dove and alighting on him. And a voice from heaven said, "This is my Son, whom I love; with him I am well pleased" (Matt 3:16-17).

This passage has two elements which need exploration: heaven opening up and the voice from heaven.

Firstly, it ought to be noted that Jesus asked John the Baptist to baptise him, one verse prior. John asked why he should do this since Jesus was the son of God. Jesus responded that it was to 'fulfil all righteousness' (Matt 3:15).

In reality, this was a declaration and a symbol of Jesus' mission to humankind. The baptism was an acceptance of the role that Jesus agreed to undertake. That is why the 'heavens opened up' once the deed was done. The clouds were separated by the craft as it descended.

A being, Jesus' father, called out below which John and his nearby disciples would have heard. Since UFOs were not understood by first century Palestinians, the belief was held that it was God who called out that "this is my Son…" (Matt 3:17).

Note that the "spirit of God descended like a dove". I argue that this was a beam of light from the craft as it acknowledged Jesus' acceptance of his role. Like a binding contract, those who sent him recognised his submission. From that moment on, he knew what he had to do and it was officially a mandatory task. The word for spirit which is used is παράκλητος (paraclete) which means 'advocate' or 'helper'. So it was an advocate or helper of God that descended from the sky.

Many Christians are adamant that the language used is metaphorical. Most commentaries since 1997 have asserted that the author(s) were putting onus upon the radiance of Christ and his being rather than using literal language.

However, this isn't necessarily the case. The authors of the gospels are happy to explicate mishaps and banal details in explicit detail which contribute little to theology. It is my conviction that this is a narrative describing physical events. The baptism need not be a completely metaphysical or mystic event.

The mystification of the baptism is wrapped in with the idea of the trinity which is a much later development in Christian theology. I believe that we have been provided with a clue into the true identity of Jesus at moments like these in the gospel accounts.

One slight difference in baptism accounts occurs in John's gospel. Instead of using the phrase 'this is my son' (Matt 3:17; Lk 3:22; Mk 1:11), the author of John uses the term 'God's Chosen One' (Jn 1:34). This phrase is a parallel of the same usage found in the book of Isaiah.

The author is once more suggesting that Jesus was selected and chosen for his role as he who was sent to earth. The event of the ascension will be elaborated upon in the second half of this book.

Parables

Now that the start and end of Jesus' earthly life have been addressed, I deem it most appropriate to tackle the central aspects of his actual mission.

Jesus so often speaks using allegories and parables. The ones which are often cited as significant are found in Matthew 13. These parables explicate two significant aspects of Jesus: how humans were created and where he came from. Jesus said these words when he was sat by the side of a lake (Matt 13:1). When he noticed crowds of people gather, he 'got into a boat and sat in it' (13:2).

Let us start with analysing the first parable that he told.

"A farmer went out to sow his seed. As he was scattering the seed, some fell along the path, and the birds came and ate it up. Some fell on rocky places, where it did not have much soil.

It sprang up quickly, because the soil was shallow. But when the sun came up, the plants were scorched, and they withered because they had no root. Other seed fell among thorns, which grew up and choked the plants. Still other seed fell on good soil, where it produced a crop - a hundred, sixty or thirty times what was sown. Whoever has ears, let them hear" (Matt 13: 3-9).

This parable is noteworthy. It's the first parable Jesus tells the crowd. There is a very good reason for this. He is speaking about the beginning or creation. The entire parable denotes the creator (the farmer) who tried to create life three times. The first time, he failed because the terrain was inhabitable (the rocky places). The second time, the same thing happened. The third time, life succeeded and grew rapidly.

This story is uncanny to say the very least. Does this farmer sound like an omnipotent God? Not in the slightest. Why would Jesus tell a story about how life came about by God and in that same story have God be incapable of creating in a perfect manner the first time around?

The parable literally maintains that through trial and error, life emerged.

In the four abductee cases that I have studied by claimants who believed they were taken by and spoken to by extraterrestrials, all had similar stories. Their accounts unanimously held the belief that aliens were responsible for human DNA and intellect. These beings who once subtly manipulated homo evolution, did so once they found appropriate conditions for life similar to that of their plant.

In 2006, NASA declared that if a habitable planet with similar conditions to earth was discovered, implanting any form of life would be a process that could take decades through trial and error.

This is the image that emerges with the parable of the sower in the above scriptural passage. Jesus is telling of how life came about on earth and where origins lie.

Jesus goes into further detail about the creation of the world in one of proceeding parables of Matthew 13.

"He told them still another parable: "The kingdom of heaven is like yeast that a woman took and mixed into about sixty pounds of flour until it worked all through the dough."

Jesus spoke all these things to the crowd in parables; he did not say anything to them without using a parable. So was fulfilled what was spoken through the prophet:

"I will open my mouth in parables, I will utter things hidden since the creation of the world" (Matt 13: 31-35).

In this parable, Jesus compares his home planet to ingredients which are the basis for making dough. He uses the exact measurement of sixty pounds of flour. This is a deliberate quantity and cultural context is very important in understanding why this measurement is so precise.

Bible scholars estimate that one pound equals one loaf. Therefore, sixty pounds would yield a total of sixty loaves of bread. Jesus is claiming something which no person could do alone, especially with the cooking technology available to Palestinians in the first century. The allusion to this exact amount of flour for the purpose of baking is not unique to Matthew. Readers of the Bible are reminded of a previous mention in Genesis 18. Interestingly, in this passage, Abraham is visited by three strangers for whom Sarah prepares cakes which use three measures of flour (Gen 18:6).

What relevance does this have in line with Jesus describing the kingdom of heaven? In using this image, he actually is making two statements about the likeness of his home: the social climate of his home planet and how the planet will be made known to human kind in the future. Let's address each of these statements respectively. Feeding is such a decisive element of the teaching of Jesus. Nurture and care comes with this connotation.

In the first instance, Jesus is describing how the seemingly impossible act of never-ending supply of love and nurture is a reality on his home planet. Both Däniken and Rael have claimed that our Creators would have found solutions to the problems we have on earth: notably in this case: sustainable development and world peace. Jesus is promising a home for those who are broken, hungry and poor. Something which he does on many occasions in the gospels (most evident in the sermon on the mount in Matt 5-7).

Secondly, Jesus makes a statement about how the Kingdom will be revealed to mankind. Notice how each parable uses a process which has a primary cause. This is either a farmer, a master, a cook, and in this parable, a baker. This cause generates a process which produces visible produce through hard work. Jesus is making the claim that his Kingdom will be made known in the end.

Just like a baker cannot see the beauty of a fully formed loaf in the initial baking process, we cannot visibly see the Kingdom or experience it in this world. We are the process. Our deeds are the ones which will save us or be our termination in the end.

If we are to be saved, we will be able to profit from those loaves which will feed us in endless supplies.

Kingdom of Heaven

Thus far, there has been a lot of reference to the Kingdom of Heaven. While I have briefly dabbled in the discussion, let me explicitly outline what the Kingdom actually is.

When you read the Bible, there is no mention of an afterlife in the Old Testament. The idea comes uniquely from the New Testament teachings of Jesus and of course Paul in his epistles. Specifically, it is referred to as the Kingdom of Heaven (particularly in Matthew as the author did not want to use the word 'God' to prevent blasphemy) or the Kingdom of God. It is specifically named first in Mark 1:14-15. It is considered to be the focal aspect of Jesus' message: that those who do good deeds and believe in Him as the son of God will attain a reality beyond this life.

My argument is that this reality is not and can not be a metaphysical one. Rather, it is completely real. Jesus is referring to his home planet which he was sent from. Jesus never clearly explains the Kingdom in a "this is what it looks like" sort of fashion.

This becomes frustrating for a lay reader who is presented with endless parables which make no immediate sense or have any relevance to the rest of the teachings of Jesus. I will not deny the fact that many of the allusions to the Kingdom are spiritual ones. Jesus obviously on some level believed that the

Kingdom was an internal reality. However, this is not unanimously true when studying the gospels in their entirety.

If the Kingdom was just an internal reality or a similar concept to nirvana in Buddhism and Hinduism, Jesus would not use phrases like "my Father in Heaven", "where I have come from", "he who is already in Heaven", "your Father who is in secret" and so on (see Matt 6:4-8, 6:26-32, Lk 12:30-32, Gal 4:6, Jn 8:42). Throughout the New Testament, readers are given the impression that the Kingdom is dual, both internal and external. One would be correct in saying that Jesus really meant to say that while the Kingdom exists as a physical place, it is similar enough to earth to be experienced on a micro level during our mortal time here.

We know that if the extraterrestrial theory is credible, then earth must have the same or similar conditions to our creators which explains why they relate to us through Jesus and vice versa.

Jesus' Truth

Jesus struggled to convince others of who he was. This is a large part of the speculation that he was an extraterrestrial because no matter how he said it, none of his disciples or the authorities fully comprehended what he was attempting to portray with his language.

Just like many other ancient astronaut theorists, it is my belief that it would seem very strange that Jesus was merely claiming to be the son of God.

Returning back to the second motive in the previous chapter for why an experiment might have been in place to create a human-hybrid, in Rael's book, he mentions Jesus' failure to convince the disciples of who he really was. Across every gospel narrative, Jesus was immensely frustrated with the inferior intellect of others who scarcely understood what he was saying (Mk 8:21).

While such a sentiment is occasionally expressed in the synoptic gospels, you only have to read a few verses of the gospel of John to know that Jesus had a difficult time making the Jewish authorities (namely the Pharisees and Sadducees) believe what he meant when he self-proclaimed his authority.

In fact, the writer of John's gospel has Jesus use the phrase 'I am telling you the truth' on seven unique occasions: Jn 3:5-7; 3:3-15; 6:26-50; 13:20-21; 10:1-21; 5:24; 16:20-25.

This sort of persuasion is unique to John's gospel and demonstrates a sense of struggle. Out of the occasions that I have listed, one verse which I will focus on is Jn 16: 23-25 (using the New International Version).

The passage reads:

"In that day you will no longer ask me anything. Very truly I tell you, my Father will give you whatever you ask in my name. Until now you have not asked for anything in my name. Ask and you will receive, and your joy will be complete.

Though I have been speaking figuratively, a time is coming when I will no longer use this kind of language but will tell you plainly about my Father."

Let us centralise our attention on two aspects: the language the writer has Jesus use and the idea of an impending 'time'.

What should strike a reader about this passage in the first instance, is the way that Jesus is clearly concealing the nature of his Father. It is almost done in a condescending manner as he implies particularly in the last verse (16:25) that he has to use figurative language to express the truth, otherwise he would not be understood.

How does the idea of Jesus being an extraterrestrial in the Raelian sense hold up against this verse? Actually, surprisingly well. A large aspect of Raelian thought is the concept that the Day of the Lord/

Day of Judgement is a metaphor for the day humans will face their creators and learn the truth. In this passage, Jesus uses 'in that day' and 'a time is coming' to denote the parousia (coming of the Lord/second coming/end times).

While Biblical scholars are generally in accordance that this is just another demonstration of Jesus being an apocalyptic preacher, our perspective cannot and should not be a Christian one.

As aforementioned numerous times, removing any preconceptions is vital to coming close to understanding the text. While we don't know the intention that the author(s) of the Gospel of John had, we need to take a refreshing new approach: looking at the canon of the New Testament as a whole with no assumptions about Jesus or who he was.

"My Father in Heaven"

It is one thing to speculate where Jesus came from and who this "Father" of his was, but what must be examined is the relationship he had with this being he called 'Abba' meaning father (Mk 14:36).

Jesus had a close relationship with the one who sent him. He refers to his father countless times across the gospels. While it is assumed in most Abrahamic faiths that this father of his was indeed the same God who spoke with Moses, Abraham, Ezekiel and all of the prophets and prophetesses of the Ancient Israelite past, our view in this book is that it was most likely the craft that was keeping a close eye on his mission, or more directly, his father.

The primary reason for this belief is that Jesus bizarrely refused to communicate directly with his father in public or even when in the presence of the twelve. We know that he "often withdrew to lonely places to pray" (Lk 5:16) and would ensure to "rise very early in the morning while it was still dark" (Mk 1:35) to speak with his father. While the nature of his relationship with 'God' will be explored to a further extent in the next chapter, the secretiveness of Jesus is fascinating and ought to be elaborated upon.

Why didn't Jesus just talk to God in front of the disciples if there was nothing to hide? Evidently, Jesus was keeping something very hidden from those he was close to. If this father was an invisible deity, why did he have to retreat to hidden places.

There are two vital Biblical verses which back up my claim.

"No one has seen Him at any time" (Jn 1:18).

"The Father who has sent me…you have neither heard His voice at any time nor seen His true form" (Jn 5:37).

For any reader and student of the Bible, these verses in John's gospel should sound very familiar. In fact, God, or Yahweh is described as 'unseen' and 'unknown' on numerous occasions in the Old Testament (Isa 47:10, Job 24:15, Gen 23:4). Most notably:

"You cannot see my face, for no man will be able to see me and at the same time, live!" (Exod 33:20).

Whenever 'God' is portrayed in this manner, one cannot help but feel that something is being concealed. Something which man cannot handle or be able to understand. Especially in the aforementioned verse in the book of Exodus, Yahweh makes the threat that no-one can see him without dying. If Yahweh was part of the creator species and was in fact an extraterrestrial, is it possible that these words were spoken to throw off and frighten early Israelites less they find out the truth about who their deity was?

You must remember that in Ancient Israel (see: Exodus 26), Yahweh physically lived in a tent which only anointed priests and Moses could enter. Threats were made to others who tried approaching. In my opinion, it makes little sense that an all-powerful God would communicate in this manner to humankind when he could simply remain concealed and invisible. Yet, throughout the Bible, he seems so real and is personified in a way which makes him appear as a spy.

The same logic applies to when he tells multiple prophets to meet him at physical locations (Hag 1:8, Mic 4:2, Exod 19:20, Exod 24:15, Isa 2:3, Deut 10:1).

The question is therefore, was this the same secret that Jesus was keeping from the disciples? That God was actually an extraterrestrial/group of extraterrestrials guiding him and providing him instructions just like they did with Moses and the ancient prophets?

There is no tangible reason why an invisible, omnipresent God would need to speak to his apostles in this manner. By nature, in Christian theology, God can do the impossible. Therefore, if Yahweh / the father of Jesus was really a God in the true sense of the word, all he would need is to implant a thought or instruction in the mind of his adherents. No location, hiddenness or secrecy would be required.

4

In 1945, near the Egyptian town of Nag Hammadi, a local farmer discovered a collection of over fifty manuscripts which are attributed to early Christians and the gnostics: an ancient religion which claimed that through 'gnosis' (knowledge), one could be saved from the evil of this lesser world.

These documents make up the Nag Hammadi library.

Some of these codices were gnostic Christian texts: texts written by communities which claimed Jesus as their own messiah and viewed him completely differently to the Jesus of orthodox Christianity. The gnostic gospels and texts are said to contain secrets about the hidden identity of Jesus.

These documents were rejected as heresy when the New Testament was being compiled and thrown away in hopes that no Christian would get his or her hands on them. The Church, in particular Irenaeus of Lyons deemed these works harmful to the doctrines which were established and countered Christian theology.

In these texts, Jesus is presented in such a different light to the gospels of the Bible. Some texts claim that he faked his own death while others sustain that Judas Iscariot was actually a saviour figure who played a vital role in salvation. Still, other texts claim that Jesus was evil as a child and grew up to use his powers for good.

The sheer multitude of the faces of Jesus in the Nag Hammadi library render a reader confused and unsure of what to believe in terms of the true identity of Jesus.

One consistency is found: that Jesus had secret gnosis (knowledge) which only the closest followers were told about. In this chapter, I will dive into two particular gnostic texts: The Secret Revelation of John and the Gospel of Thomas.

The Secret Revelation of John

I will first present an extract to you so that you might get a clear picture of what is being dealt with:

"One day when John the brother of James, the sons of Zebedee, went up to the temple, it happened that a Pharisee named Arimanios came up to him and said to him,

'Where is your teacher, whom you followed?'

I said to him, 'He has returned to the place from which he came.' The Pharisee said to me, 'This Nazarene (Jesus) has deceived you badly, filled your ears with lies, closed your minds, and turned you from the traditions of your parents.'

When I, John, heard this, I turned away from the temple and went to a mountainous and barren place. I was distressed within, and I said,

'How was the saviour (Jesus) selected?

Why was he sent into the world by his father?

Who is his father who sent him?

To what kind of eternal realm shall we go?

And what was he saying when he told us, This eternal realm to which you will go is modelled after the incorruptible everlasting realm, but he did not teach us what kind of realm that one is?'

At the same moment that I thought about this, the sky opened up, all creation beneath lit up brightly, and the ground shook.

I was afraid and I saw within the light a child standing by me. As I was staring, it seemed to be an elderly person. Again it changed its appearance to be a young person.

Not that there were several figures before me. Rather, there was a figure with several forms within the light. These forms appeared through each other, and the figure had three forms.

The figure said to me,

'Oh John, John! Why are you doubting? Why are you afraid? Are you not familiar with this person? Then do not be fainthearted. I am with you always. I am the father, I am the mother, I am the child. I am the incorruptible and the undefiled one.

Now I have come to teach you what is, what was, and what is to come, that you may understand what is invisible and what is visible; and to teach you about the unshakable race of perfect humankind. So now, lift up your head that you may understand the things I shall tell you today, and that you may relate them to your spiritual friends, who are from the unshakable race of perfect humankind'" (Meyer, 2003).

The narrative in this first part of the story in The Secret Revelation of John resembles the kind of imagery that we saw in the Ascension scene in the book of Acts. Extremely graphic imagery is present throughout. For the sake of clarity, it would convene one to break down what is happening in this passage.

The text concerns John the apostle. He was the son of Zebedee and the younger brother of James the Greater. Both brothers were the disciples of John the Baptist before they were told to follow Jesus. They were both part of the twelve disciples and had very close ties with Jesus during his earthly life.

The story begins during a time supposedly before the destruction of the temple in Jerusalem. He was walking towards it when one of Jesus' enemies and opposers to the first Christian movement, Arimanios appears to taunt him. He asks where Jesus is and John answers that he has returned to the 'place from which he came'.

After Arimanios spits hatred at John and insults the authority of Jesus, John, now distressed and upset, hides away at mountain top in a hidden place. He doubts everything Jesus told him and asks a series of questions.

Why did Jesus come into the world? Who was his father? Where is the place which he came from where we will go one day? Once he asked these questions, the sky above opens and the clouds part. A beam of light shines down and whatever caused the sky to open also causes the ground to shake. A person appears who John cannot clearly see. This being reassures John that he is not alone and that by seeing the true face of the 'imperishable one', he might be assured of his belief in who Jesus was and where he came from.

Needless to say, this revelation is one of the strongest pieces of manuscript evidence from the second century which depicts something extraterrestrial. My conviction seems affirmed with the description of the events which take place.

Notice how yet again, the craft appears when the person in question (in this case John) is in secret and in 'a barren place'.

The way in which the reveal occurs before John's eyes is similar to Ezekiel's vision of God. I believe that what is being described can only be a UFO encounter. The clearing in the clouds, the ground trembling, the light beam from the headlights of the craft and who is inside of it.

It is uncannily reminiscent of the ascension scene. It's almost as though the ascension is being re-performed before the eyes of one of Jesus' disciples in order to show him that what he believes to be true is in fact veritable at a time when a witness to Jesus' life begins to doubt what had happened.

Everything matches up with the extraterrestrial theory which Jesus is affiliated with. At this point, I could enquire into other gnostic texts which contain UFO-esque imagery but that would not be useful since this text illustrates with utmost coherence and explicitness the most clear UFO sighting in the gnostic library.

The Gospel of Thomas

The Gospel of Thomas is an unusual document. Numerous scholars disagree with the fact that it is grouped among the gnostic gospels since the entire book is a conversation between Jesus and his disciples. Moreover, it is almost purely a list of his sayings and philosophical teachings with only three lines of narration.

The basic formula found in this gospel is as follows: a disciple asks a question, Jesus replies and the disciple responds to the answer.

Within these sayings and traditions, there are a handful which aid in the Jesus extraterrestrial theory. The first which will be looked at is taken from verse 15.

"When you see one who was not born of woman, fall on your faces and worship. That one is your Father."

Here, Jesus reveals who the father is. He expresses it in the most forward manner: that the one who is his father is the one who isn't a human i.e. not born of a woman. Jesus heavily implies that this being will be seen one day ('when') and has physical form. Nowhere in the Bible are we presented with such a simplistic view of Yahweh. While it could be argued that Jesus is describing an eternal deity, the way in which the gospel of Thomas is presented suggests that he is talking in physical terms. This brings us onto the next verse which I will discuss which shows how Jesus is attempting to convince his disciples of the nature of his father.

"If they (the unbelievers) ask you, 'What is the evidence of your Father in you?' say to them, 'It is motion and rest.'"

Jesus is commanding his followers about what to say to those who do not believe when they ask about what proof exists that believers have the essence of Father within them. His response is telling "motion and rest".

The very fact that we move in our daily lives as creatures and at the end of the day, we slumber in repose is sufficient evidence of our likeness to our Creators. Jesus' answer is surprising. From the canonical gospels, one would assume that his answer would be to do with the Holy Spirit or the presence of God within a person and yet, he settles for something physical and elementary: that we move and rest just like his father. Jesus is presenting the truth that we were protected and governed by creatures who made us in their own likeness. His father is one of these and the one who sent him.

There is a verse in the gospel of Thomas which depicts the planetary home of Jesus and its likeness i.e. the Kingdom of Heaven. Jesus is asked what it is like and his response is:

"For there are five trees in Paradise for you; they do not change, summer or winter, and their leaves do not fall. Whoever knows them will not taste death."

Jesus is alluding to the paradise which is the place in which he came from. While prominent academics have argued that this saying is a reference to the tree of life in the garden of Eden (see: Gen 1-3), I would argue that these five trees are metaphorical symbols for some kind of innovation, medicine or knowledge which humanity at the time of the writing of the gospel of Thomas did not comprehend. This could be immortality, true knowledge or something similar. Whatever it is, it is unchanging and permanent. Jesus promises health and eternal life in the place he calls home. This is consistent with many testimonies of abductees who make the claim of advanced scientific knowledge.

Finally, a verse from Thomas' gospel which affirms Jesus' identity and relation to his father and the Creator species.

"You examine the face of heaven and earth, but you have not come to know the one who is in your presence, and you do not know how to examine the present moment."

Jesus explains that mankind has looked across the earth and up into the sky to find truth about who God is but in reality, 'the one who is in your presence' is what they were looking for all along. Once more, Jesus proclaims his identity as part of the father. Just like he stated in John 14:7, by knowing him, one knows who the father is since they are in the same likeness and of the same kind.

5

Based on all the evidence in scripture, one thing is made very plain, that Jesus countlessly tried to convince others of his identity and unsurprisingly, nobody grasped this truth. Perhaps, he came during the wrong time in human history. First century Judaism was obsessed with Jewish law and following every commandment of the Torah for the most part. How different would history have been if those early followers knew about UFOs and extraterrestrial life? Would we even have bothered to form a religion based on this man called the Christ?

To that extent, what are the implications for Jesus being an extraterrestrial? Should Christians no longer pray? Is there no God? I would answer no to both these questions because ultimately, everything in this book is speculation.

At this point in our history, alternative theories are needed and ought to be taken seriously. We are passed the point that we were in throughout the

1980s and 90s where anything to do with aliens was far-fetched. We should be passed the point of imagining a dumb stoner when talks about abduction arise. Yet we aren't and that is the biggest shame that is holding us back from exploring the depths of the unknown.

As a species, it is time to move on from the dark ages of knowledge which are holding us back from digging deeper into the truth. Everyone, whether spiritual, religious or secular wants to know the truth. The truth which binds us, the truth about where we came from and about where we are headed. Human beings possess the capacity to go beyond our own nature and inquire further. We can go against our own instincts, question them, debate them. We can build civilisations and be extraordinarily creative but simultaneously be destructive, oppressive and regressive.

While religion has brought about innovations in culture, art, music, and has provided solace to those who are in pain, something novel is required.

People are happy to stay in the dark and not know about things. Jesus taught that 'those who have ears, let them hear'. Ironically, only a handful of believers do this.

Most Christians haven't read the Bible and yet for some reason, people are happy to believe in a deity who is inconsistent but are not willing to believe in the very real possibility that we were visited and influenced by a similar species to our own thousands of years ago.

While my mind tells me to have hope in humanity, there is a great portion of it which tells me that we are not ready for the truth and humanity is not allowing itself to advance beyond the old order of the world. The order which relied on superstition, blind faith, and experiences which are make-believe and are entirely caused by brain chemistry.

That is why I maintain that Jesus being an extraterrestrial is mere speculation. I will not dare to say that he was or wasn't with certainty because while I personally believe this to be true, I try to have an open mind.

If one day, those who came to our earth in ancient times do in fact make a return and it is proven that Jesus of Nazareth was an extraterrestrial, how would that change things? Indispensably, it would undoubtedly be the most significant discovery in human history and yet, those same people who wrote conspiracy theorists off as lunatics would be the first to lie and claim that they knew all along.

PART 2

THE ASCENSION

6

In this second part of the book, we're going to be looking at the ascension of Christ. I believe that it merits its own respective section instead of being grouped in with other elements of his life and story because it is simply the most fascinating. For Christians the world over, the account of the ascension as told by Luke in the synoptic gospel and in the book of Acts has played a pivotal role in the development of Christian theology and in the beliefs that make up the Christian religion in its many denominations.

I'm not going to be taking the exegetical approach though and when examining the ascension, I'm going to be a lot more literal. Now, as a disclaimer, I understand how there are various philosophical, spiritual and theological interpretations of the accounts but for the sake of speculation, I will admit that I am going to be a lot more literal. Make of that what you will.

Just as Jesus came into our world in a mysterious manner, he exited it in an even more bizarre manner. The ascension of Christ has been a focal part of Biblical academia since the twelfth century. However, we have been deprived of a logical or physical explanation for the event. Every commentary (both secular and conservative) that I have come across sustains that the belief in Jesus' ascension is a matter of faith and that the Church has contended with the story since the time of Irenaeus. But Irenaeus and the development of doctrine surrounding Jesus' death and ascension came much later than the writings of the New Testament.

The authors of the gospels and the book of Acts did not have doctrine in mind. They were telling a narrative which started out as an oral tradition from early followers. When you strip away 'Christianity' from the story, you finally arrive at the perspective that the writers originally wanted to put across: that factually, Jesus went into heaven on a cloud.

How come the ascension is even mentioned if it was not a physical manifestation? From the scriptural evidence, it is apparent what the early believers in Jesus knew to be true:

"He was taken up before their very eyes, and a cloud hid him from their sight.

They were looking intently up into the sky as he was going, when suddenly two men dressed in white stood beside them. "Men of Galilee," they said, "why do you stand here looking into the sky? This same Jesus, who has been taken from you into heaven, will come back in the same way you have seen him go into heaven" (Acts 1:6-11).

- -

When I was an undergraduate at college, I asked my professor the two questions which all new readers of this passage in the book of Acts has.

Who were the two men dressed in white?

Did Jesus literally go up into heaven?

His answer was completely wishy-washy, for lack of a better term. This passage is hard to theologise and yet scholars, especially those of faith want to add so many dimensions to the narrative to distract you of the very strange story being told.

The Greek in this passage clearly uses literal language that two men wearing white presided over Jesus as he was taken up into a cloud and into the sky (heaven). That is it! No fairy tale of a holy spirit or God creating illusions and making it look like Jesus was being transported.

That is what the Church wants Christians to believe because anything weird or suspicious must be explained using their best defence: faith. But faith has never proven anything archaeologically or historically. They hate writers and skeptics who question them. But that's exactly what I am doing here. We have these accounts in the New Testament which make a claim. We don't need or require belief in God to help explain it.

The ascension narrative is fascinating. Reading it is beautifully wonderful and yet, I would maintain that like the baptism, it holds the secret of Jesus' identity. I would dare go even further to argue that it is the most convincing passage in any ancient manuscript which depicts a UFO.

It's just a bonus that it happens to be associated with Jesus.

Let's look at what the passage is saying in closer detail. At two points, the writer clarifies that the disciples were stunned by the sight. This is demonstrated by the use of the word 'intently' (Acts 1:6). The men in white who watched over even spoke to them asking them why they were in awe. They say, "this same Jesus being taken from you" (Acts 1:10-11) because the disciples probably couldn't believe their eyes.

What we are dealing with in this story is Jesus being taken up on a craft (called a 'cloud' because UFOs were not known back then) after his mission was complete. Two members of his species (the men in white) settle the minds of the disciples that he will one day return as they ensure Jesus' safety as he ascends back to his home planet.

Critically, it would not be erroneous to consider this a leap but how else might one interpret the story? The Jesus extraterrestrial theory thrives throughout the gospel narrative. The It follows nicely at every parable, journey, teaching and event. In particular, our greatest evidence are the beginnings and endings of his earthly life. I will break down a simplified comparison between the Christian narrative of Jesus and the extraterrestrial narrative of the same story.

Christian Narrative:

A virgin called Mary was implanted with the seed of God at a random point in history so that she might give birth to the long awaited Jewish Messiah. the half God child is born, baptised and later performs miracles. Throughout his mission, a holy spirit follows him and blesses him. He is arrested for blasphemy, is crucified and rises from the dead. He remains for three days and then is taken up to heaven by God to remain until the final days.

Extraterrestrial Narrative:

The creator species realised that the Jewish population who they chose as their people (two thousand years prior) were in need of a renewal of contact. The species believed that it was an appropriate time to make actual contact but could not do so 100% authentically since mankind was not yet ready.

They decided that a human hybrid would possess the capacity to empathise humanly all the while possessing the advanced spiritual and scientific knowledge to teach humanity about their origins, forgiveness and advanced level of ethics. This was the true dual nature of Jesus.

The 'Father' of Jesus implanted his sperm into Mary in her sleep (Matt 1:24-25) and the child was born. He was tested by the creators in the desert to ensure he was prepared for his mission and wouldn't let them down (Matt 4:1-11).

When he had passed the test, he began to teach about who he was, where he had come from and how to live a better ethical life. This is with the promise of immortality and rejuvenation for the good which the creator species seemingly mastered on their planet. This is the Kingdom which Jesus speaks of where the chosen will live after death.

Jesus was then arrested for blasphemy, chose Peter to carry on the message and then might have been crucified . Afterwards, he was saved by advanced scientific methodology and was taken back to his home planet once his mission was complete.

Both narratives require some deep investigation and belief but the Christian narrative has the most problems. Theology and metaphysical beliefs are required for interpretation which muddies the stories beyond recognition. For instance, why did Jesus need to be tempted if an all-knowing God sent him? Why was Jesus a man? Why was he flawed? Why did God send a spirit and two men in white? Why didn't the disciples recognise him after his resurrection? And so on. The extraterrestrial narrative is consistent and explains much better the mysteries surrounding Jesus, even if it is considered just as far-fetched. We can conceive of aliens arriving on earth but using empirical evidence and perhaps logic, we cannot conceive of a deity adopting a semi-human/semi-God to perform miracles and suffering the way Jesus did.

At this point, you might argue that the ascension is an anomaly and that it is only held by one cultural and religious affiliation. It is not. The ascension by physical means is also described in the Noble Qur'an.

In Islam, it is a fact that Jesus was not crucified but it was only made to appear that he was. Instead, he was taken up to heaven.

"And [for] their saying, "Indeed, we have killed the Messiah, Jesus (السلام عليكم), the son of Mary, the messenger of Allah ." And they did not kill him, nor did they crucify him; but [another] was made to resemble him to them.

And indeed, those who differ over it are in doubt about it. They have no knowledge of it except the following of assumption. And they did not kill him, for certain...But Allah took him up unto Himself." (Surah An-Nisa 4:157).

Whether the Holy prophet of Islam was told the story directly by an angel or not, the story of the ascension of Jesus clearly made its way across the Near and Middle East by 1400.

It is even more interesting how no theologising is made in either religious texts. Just like in the book of Acts, the Qur'an tells the story as a hard fact without adding mystical elements which would render the story a question of faith. Both narratives are in accordance that Jesus was physically taken from a position of terrestrial dwelling up into the sky somewhere.

As far as I know, heaven is not a physical location and so Jesus must have been taken somewhere outside of our planet and by the means of some craft. I will posit wholeheartedly that this place is the place of his Father: the Kingdom from which he came. The means of travel: a UFO.

7

Let us slow things down a bit though. I understand that this is a lot to state and claim without much evidence so I want to take a deeper look at the ascension, with specific focus on the accounts in the gospels of Luke and John. The passages or rather, chapters concerned are Luke 24 and John 20. These are honestly a fascinating parts of the New Testament and some which are intriguing for all readers, be they Christian, secular, or otherwise. Not all of chapter is necessarily relevant to the ascension and to the speculation that Jesus was taken up into the skies by a UFO and so I will only draw upon appropriate verses in this chapter. Nonetheless, it is a great read and I would highly recommend that if you have a moment, to read the entirety of the verse. You can find it   online on the website 'Bible Gateway'.

Without further ado, let's look at some excerpts from Luke 24 and John 20 and then analyse what they might be saying from a UFO and ancient astronaut theorist point of view.

"On the first day of the week, very early in the morning, the women took the spices they had prepared and went to the tomb. They found the stone rolled away from the tomb, but when they entered, they did not find the body of the Lord Jesus." (Lk 24:1-3).

"He is not here; he has risen!" (Lk 24:6).

"Now that same day two of them were going to a village called Emmaus, about seven miles from Jerusalem. They were talking with each other about everything that had happened. As they talked and discussed these things with each other, Jesus himself came up and walked along with them; but they were kept from recognising him." (Lk 24:13-16).

"When he had led them out to the vicinity of Bethany, he lifted up his hands and blessed them. While he was blessing them, he left them and was taken up into heaven. Then they worshiped him and returned to Jerusalem with great joy. And they stayed continually at the temple, praising God." (Lk 24:50-53).

Now, there are a few interesting points here for us to examine. Let's begin.

The Empty Tomb

In the morning on the first day of the week, Jesus' mother, Mary Magdalene and Joanna went to visit the tomb of Jesus. This was out of reverence and as blessing. (In case you're wondering who Joanna is, she was a woman who accompanied the twelve disciples and Jesus on their travels, helping them and supporting their cause.)

What they noticed, upon reaching the tomb is that the stone that covered the cave had been rolled away, meaning that someone had moved it. If you want a visual of this, you merely have to look at the front cover of this book. They rushed in only to discover that the body of Jesus was gone. Later, when they asked about what might have happened, they were told that he had 'risen'.

At this point, an extract from John 20 complements the narrative almost perfectly and provides more insight and information than any other source. The passage concerned can be found in Jn 20:11-18 and it is here where as Mary Magdalene is crying in the empty tomb having assumed someone had stolen her saviour's body, two 'angels in white' appear to her (Jn 20:12). After asking her why she's crying, she tells them that she's worried that someone stole the body of Jesus.

As she's saying this, she turns around and sees Jesus standing right behind her but she 'did not realise that it was Jesus' (Jn 20:14). Mary thought that is was the gardener and requested that these angels tell her where they put Jesus' body. This is when Jesus calls her name and she turns around and replies with the Aramaic word for 'teacher' (Jn 20:16).

Up until now, the story hasn't been too alien-esque but this is the moment where there is a shift. Mary tries to reach out her hand to Jesus but he tells her,

"Do not hold on to me, for I have not yet ascended" (Jn 20:17).

So what does the story of the empty tomb teach us about the essence of Jesus' extraterrestrial nature? Two things certainly stand out in my mind.

1. The angels in white which we also saw in Acts.
2. Jesus' words 'do not hold on to me, for I have not yet ascended'.

We sufficiently talked about the angels in white in the previous chapter so I really want to focus on what Jesus says in John 20:17. Many Christians hold firm to the idea that the resurrection was entirely spiritual and had a metaphysical aspect to it that makes it impossible to speak about is physical terms. My problem with this is - then why are so many descriptions of his ascension physical. We saw in the book of Acts how Jesus was taken up by a cloud that promised to return him to earth some day, and now Jesus tells Mary to not hold on to him. If the event was spiritual, why would Mary touching him impede his journey into heaven? Jesus would not have demanded that she not touch him unless doing so would prevent him from ascending. Let me use a very menial and every day example to explain my point. Let's say that you are trying to get into a car. As you put your right leg in and start to move your body so that you might enter the vehicle, someone grabs your other leg and stops you from achieving your aim.

In such a moment, what do you do? The logical person would request that the other person let go so that you can complete the manoeuvre to get in the car. Now, let us assume that it is not your physical body that is entering the car but rather, your soul. Any adherent of a faith that believes in the eternal soul (such as Christians would hold to the spiritual ascension) happens to believe the soul is not physical and cannot be touched. Any attempt to 'grab' your soul to impede it from entering the car would be futile because the soul is not physical. This, while a very silly example, can be applied to the logic of Jesus' words.

Why would Jesus have told Mary not to hold onto him unless doing so would have prevented him from rising? I'm sure there are many theological analyses of this verse and I myself have looked into them a little bit. While they lean a lot on the idea that the synoptic gospels utilise Greek and Judaic mythology and ideas about the soul, life after death and a return to the divine realm, they do not satisfy the appetite of those who disbelieve in the soul and those who crave actual explanations outside of the realm of spirituality.

In my view, based on not only this source but the accounts of the gnostic gospels, Jesus was taken up into a craft and in John's account, he was being lifted after his body was restored by the Ones who took him up. That's why he didn't want Mary to touch him as he was in the process of being sucked into the vehicle.

With regards to the angels, I'm astounded that Mary wasn't more afraid when she saw them. Throughout the Old and New Testament, angels often frighten people when they are seen and yet, Mary refers to one of them as 'Sir' (Jn 20:15) which signifies that she believed them to be humans. This might seem pretty banal and mundane, however, I'm going to make the argument that it's pretty shocking and goes hand in hand with the theory that Rael and may other proponents of ancient astronaut theory have put forward since the 1960s. This is also supported by the ancient Sumerians and Babylonians.

According to them, angels were members of our creator species and so, they are very human like and for some unexplained reason, quite short. The reason why religions, particularly those of the Abrahamic family tree mention them as divine is because they were more technologically advanced than the human civilisations who mentioned them. Since they were confused and frightened of these creatures who flew down to our planet in spacecrafts, in their minds, they were either divine Gods or messengers of God or the Gods.

This fits nicely into the empty tomb story of Luke 24 and John 20 because firstly, Mary wasn't phased nor frightened by them, and secondly, they were inside of Jesus' empty tomb. The fact that two supposedly grown human-like people were able to fit into the tomb of one person (unless Jesus was in fact ridiculously tall but this is historically inaccurate) means they were very short.

They Didn't Recognise Jesus

When two disciples who knew Jesus very well were walking along after the events of the resurrection, Jesus himself approached them. They saw him and did not recognise him until much later when he broke bread with a group of them.

I've read four different exegeses on this account and what seems to be the trend in New Testament scholarship is that either the disciples were too far away to recognise him or they were so baffled to see him because people don't tend to expect to see their dead friend, or in this case Messiah, walking along the road after the funeral. While this would make the most logical sense, I do not believe the gospel writers would have made such a big deal about this more than once in the accounts. If it was a case of the fact that they were dazed and confused, it would have been explicitly mentioned as the reason or part of the reason that they couldn't grasp the fact that Jesus was still somehow alive. But their bafflement isn't really mentioned until later in the gospel of John and in Luke too. I sincerely think that the gospel writers wanted to note that Jesus was physically different and unrecognisable.

Allow me to now bring in the alien component to this. There are three sources that support the fact that Jesus had morphed and physically transformed.

1. Paul writes a rather explicit explanation of the process of post-mortem transfiguration.

2. This wasn't the first time Jesus changed his appearance.

With regards to the first point, Paul of Tarsus who authors the epistles that constitute so much of the New Testament is seen as the authority for 90% of Christian theology and belief. He himself who persecuted Christians in the first century AD converted on a trip to Damascus when Jesus spoke to him. In his first letter to the Corinthians, he discusses in depth how our bodies transform and it isn't as vague as one might think:

"But let me reveal to you a wonderful secret. We will not all die, but we will all be transformed! It (transformation of the body) will happen in a moment, in the blink of an eye, when the last trumpet is blown. For when the trumpet sounds, those who have died will be raised to live forever. And we who are living will also be transformed. For our dying bodies must be transformed into bodies that will never die; our mortal bodies must be transformed into immortal bodies. Then, when our dying bodies have been transformed into bodies that will never perish."
(1 Cor 15:51-54)

The theology and analysis behind these verses have literally been the topic of discussion for some PhD researcher's theses. Why? Because it is such a complex idea. The passage in question draws on many influences. Paul was raised in Pharisaic tradition and also had knowledge of Greek mythology and philosophy concerning the nature of existence and the fate of the soul. Nonetheless, his assertion here about what happens to the body is entirely consistent with Jesus' after-death appearance in John and Luke.

He posits that the body we were 'given' at birth dies and perishes away and then we're given a sort of 'new skin' in the form of an imperishable body. We're transformed in 'the blink of an eye'. He speaks of the end of the world 'trumpet' sound that can be heard across the globe when the end of time draws near. Paul says that even if you're still alive at that moment, you will inherit a new body that will be suitable for the kingdom which we go to.

In spite of my own Biblical Studies training, I can't help but think of Jean Sendy and Rael's account of the kingdom of heaven where our alien ancestors dwell. The latter claimed that he was taken there on a space vessel and asserted that the planet where the 'Elohim' live is the promised place that religions believe to be 'heaven'. When we get there, if we are good, we are provided an appearance which is the most perfect and in tact. Such a concoction was devised thousands of years ago and is a reward for the good of heart.

Outside of Rael's story, the Qur'an's description of heaven/paradise is very similar with beliefs of resurrection of the body into a new form. Such a form can eat endless amounts of food without feeling satiated, is not capable of sadness and is perfect in every manner.

Whether you choose to believe that St. Paul was describing a physical transfiguration or one of spiritual essence based on what he knew of Greek mythology and the Jewish afterlife, it is fascinating conjecture in the context of UFOs and extraterrestrials.

With concerns to the second point i.e. the fact that this wasn't the first time Jesus changed his appearance, I refer you to four New Testament verses: 2 Peter 1:16-18, Luke 9:28-36, Mark 9:2-8 and Matthew 17:1-8. What do all of these passages talk about? About a rather peculiar event that occurred on top of a mountain. In front of three disciples: James, Peter, and John, Jesus' clothes turned white and his face took the form of Moses and Elijah.

While this has nothing to do with the ascension per say, it is very relevant when discussing both how Jesus can seemingly take different forms and how he is linked to the extraterrestrials who sent him to earth as an experiment. Why? Because whenever Jesus changes form, albeit after the empty tomb account or in this passage, UFO imagery is present:

"While he was speaking, a bright cloud covered them, and a voice from the cloud said 'This is my Son, whom I love; with him I am well pleased. Listen to him!'" (Matt 17:5).

This verse again signifies a 'bright cloud' that a voice came out of. Jesus had taken his disciples up on top of that mountain so that he could communicate with a space-craft of the extraterrestrials who sent him. The transfiguration into other forms (that of past prophets) was to show the disciples the ultimate power of the aliens who sent him so that they will believe that he was who he said he was. It's worth noting that these 'clouds' are always described as bright because any flying craft has to have lights. This is consistent with the **book of Ezekiel** where the prophet was visited by a UFO. For reference and if you want to read more about it, check out the book for yourself.

8

We're going to take a break from the Biblical side of things for a while. In this chapter, I'm going to be discussing a different aspect of the 'Jesus was an alien' claim - painters in history who knew, or rather, had a hunch that Jesus wasn't exactly the man from Nazareth that the majority of people thought he was. I will also touch upon Da Vinci and the secrets that he knew.

Jesus the Extraterrestrial in Art

If someone of this day and age painted a scene of the New Testament with a UFO in the sky, many would mock this artist and think him/her to be a bit of a conspiracy nut with a wide imagination. The reason we'd have that reaction is because of the media age that we live in where the concept of Jesus being an extraterrestrial has existed for quite a while and isn't anything particularly 'new'. Especially with the internet age, even if a person hasn't heard of the claims that Jesus was indeed an alien, it wouldn't surprise anyone that there are groups of people out there who hold very firm to that claim and belief (the irony of me saying all of this).

However, what if someone from the fourteenth or even seventeenth century painted a scene from the New Testament with a UFO in the sky? We'd think it to be a lot more eerie and we would all take more interest in it because back then, the concept of UFOs and extraterrestrials did not even exist. Such an artist would not have much to be inspired by when in such centuries, cars didn't even exist. So what if I told you that on numerous occasions in centuries gone by, artists did actually explicitly paint Jesus being of extraterrestrial origin. In this chapter, we're going to be taking a look at three paintings:

1. The Crucifixion Of Christ (1350) - Visoki Dečani

2. The Baptism Of Christ (1710) - Aert De Gelder

3. The Madonna with Saint Giovannino (approx. late 1400s) - Domenico Ghirlandaio

Starting with *The Crucifixion of Christ* which was painted in 1350, visitors to the Visoki Decani Monastery in Kosovo come to see such a painting for one primary reason. Take a look at a picture of the painting below and see if you can work it out.

Upon first look, this is seemingly your standard Christian depiction of the crucifixion of Jesus. He is hanging on the cross with his disciples lamenting around him. Jerusalem is in the background and angels are sat in the sky around him. However, one prominent feature stands out which doesn't 'fit' in with the rest of the scenery. The two orbs on the left and right hand corners of the painting. They remarkably contrast the tone and mood of the painting which is more or less traditional. Nonetheless, these two orbs really do not have a religious meaning and experts often find it arduous to explain why Dečani placed them there. Let's take a zoomed in look at such orbs.

This is the one that sits on the left hand side of the painting and it is evident to see that there is a man who is sat in a sort of vehicle that is soaring through the sky above Jesus. This vehicle is shaped as though it has been designed for sky/space travel and even has three propelling spikes and one forward facing one too. There is a star on the vehicle as well. Nobody can say with certainty the reason why Dečani painted these odd crafts in a Jesus painting but if we're being honest, it's a creepy addition for a 1350 art piece. The interesting thing about these two creatures and the spacecrafts that it seems they are driving is that they are in no way linked to the Biblical story of the crucifixion. Dečani wouldn't have had many resources outside of the Biblical accounts we find in the gospels. So, where did he get this information from and more importantly, what was he trying to suggest by adding these?

The painting itself is quite explicit! It's clear when he's depicting holiness (with rings which are present around Jesus' head, the angels and the disciples) so one cannot make the claim that these orb like conceptions and the people inside them are just mere angels. They're something else...the only question is 'what are they' and how did he know about them? Such a mystery can only be speculated upon because the artist has long been dead and we have no records from him that explain his work.

Our second painting is *The Baptism of Christ* which was painted in 1710 by Aert De Gelder.

What draws people to this work of art is the UFO shaped disc that is shining upon Jesus and John the Baptist. Unlike Dečani, the artist of this painting De Gelder was explicit using a Biblical source which is from Matthew 3:13-17…

"Then Jesus came from Galilee to the Jordan to be baptised by John. But John tried to deter him, saying, "I need to be baptised by you, and do you come to me?" Jesus replied, "Let it be so now; it is proper for us to do this to fulfil all righteousness." Then John consented.

As soon as Jesus was baptised, he went up out of the water. **At that moment heaven was opened, and he saw the Spirit of God descending like a dove and alighting on him. And a voice from heaven said, "This is my Son, whom I love; with him I am well pleased.""**

The highlighted verse is the one which De Gelder was clearly influenced by. However, the Biblical passage says nothing about a physical presence in the sky shrining on Jesus like a car with its lights on. The author(s) of the gospel of Matthew might have been talking in imagery and the presence was spiritual. Or was he? De Gelder's work is another mystery in the same are of interest of Jesus being an extraterrestrial because he, in 1710, interpreted the passage in

Matthew much like modern-day proponents of ancient astronaut theory.

The third, and arguably most compelling piece of art that supports the Jesus-alien theory is *The Madonna with Saint Giovannino* by Domenico Ghirlandaio. This one is utterly fascinating and you'll see why in just a second. First though, take a look at the painting.

It all seems pretty normal until you look a little deeper at the man standing in the background on the shoreline. He is looking up at something in the sky…

But what exactly is he looking at? Something hovering in the sky that someone in the 1400s such as Domenico Ghirlandaio should not have been aware of. It is clearly visible that the man in the painting is looking at something above him that is capable of flight and is not a natural phenomenon. Such a thing is shining and is very much in line with what we think of as a 'UFO' or even helicopter. Both things didn't exist back then.

Okay, so there is a UFO and a man looking up at it. So what does it have to do with Jesus?

Well, the focal point of the painting is Mary and the baby Jesus. It seems that a group of painters of the Renaissance had some sort of knowledge of a link between Jesus and aliens or at the very least UFOs and highly advanced technology. It really makes you wonder and think what else they knew, how they knew such things and why nothing has been revealed since then.

Da Vinci

The relationship between Leonardo Da Vinci, Jesus and conspiracy theories has a long history in the mainstream media. However, I'm not going to be discussing anything about the Da Vinci Code and the whole theory about Jesus having a bloodline.

I'll instead focus on an element of Da Vinci that isn't really talked about enough - the fact that he hinted many times at the fact that Jesus wasn't who people thought he was. In case you're new to the controversy surrounding Da Vinci's depictions of the Christ, this painter was known for painting Jesus in controversial ways. The Church despised him (and still do). For one, he would always paint Jesus as extremely effeminate without a beard and in some cases, possessing fully developed breasts. In other of his Jesus paintings, Jesus has a cheeky grin on his face as if to say that there is more to the story than people believe. All in all, Da Vinci really knew things that the Church didn't want him to let out. How do we know this? They paid him for his silence...multiple times.

The only question is, why? And to that end, what was this secret that was too dangerous to let out into the public?

We shouldn't jump to any conclusions about what Da Vinci knew about Jesus and the Church but it is curious that he hints at bizarre things throughout his artwork. I want to take a look at one of his paintings that is chilling and signifies something more than what it lets on at first glance.

This painting is Saint John the Baptist (1513-1516), believed by experts to have been Da Vinci's last piece of art. You can find a picture of it on the next page and when you look at it, I would like you to seek out any nuance and small details. Analyse the painting well and then, I'll go into more detail about how it relates not only to Jesus as an extraterrestrial but about Da Vinci's message as a whole and secret knowledge which he knew about which could revolutionise Christianity and our understanding of the Bible and the figures which the Church has always considered holy.

Saint John the Baptist

(Leonardo Da Vinci)

This painting shows a very feminine John the Baptist pointing to the sky. If you look closely at his hand, you'll see a faint cross that resembles the crucifix of Jesus. John has curly brown hair and wide eyes.

What's particularly noteworthy is the rather disturbing and intriguing grimace on his face. He has a smirk that is both dark and suggestive. While some scholars assert that this is a look of homoeroticism that Da Vinci deliberately painted, to me it's a look that is cheeky as if to say he knows of something. It's secretive and deceptive. Just as with the other artists that have been examined, we have to ask what Da Vinci knew of John the Baptist and what contemporaries of his knew. Simply put, they knew the Biblical narrative.

In the New Testament, John the Baptist served as a prophet who was to 'make clear the path of the Lord'. One who prophesied the coming of Jesus as was he precursor in the story of the Messiah. One must remember that John the Baptist himself had disciples. He was a traveler and most likely an Essene.

The Essenes were a denomination of Judaism that existed during the time of Jesus. Little is known about them and not much is historically known about John the Baptist other than his role as prophet and the fact that he was the cousin of Jesus.

Why would Da Vinci have a vested interest in painting John the Baptist like this? My theory is that he was trying to make a provocative statement about John. Notably that he was from the upper realm - from the 'heavens'/skies and that Jesus was also from there. This explains why he is holding a cross. The smirk on John the Baptist's face says that he knows about where Jesus went.

I have another proposition, however. One which is more focused on a historical reality. This theory is centred around the idea that John the Baptist and Jesus were actually the same person and that the John that Da Vinci painted was mocking what people of Jesus' day thought about him and his identity.

There existed a group of gnostics called the Mandaeans. They're forgotten in history and honestly, their cosmological and theological beliefs are incredibly interesting. Of these beliefs, the one that stuns many scholars and readers the most is that Jesus was a fraud who was just copying John the Baptist who they believe was an authentic Messiah.

In fact, some extra-canonical sources including the gospel of Judas hint at the fact that John the Baptist was a true Messiah and that Jesus was secondary. Others state that John the Baptist and Jesus were too similar in nature and in teaching to have been distinct people. I've also heard the notion that the gospel writers deliberately fabricated one or both characters when in fact they were the same figure.

So where does the alien aspect come in? The alien element can be introduced if we are to believe that John the Baptist and Jesus were in fact the same person. Da Vinci may have believed this which explains why (a) John and Jesus look strangely similar in Da Vinci's portfolio and (b) why he is holding a cross in this painting and pointing upwards towards the sky. The sole explanation I can fathom is that John wants people to know where he came from and where Jesus ascended to.

Some recent ancient astronaut theorists have said that when you mirror this painting in a reflection, you can see the face of an alien like creature in the middle. I dismiss this entirely.

Ultimately, I might be completely wrong and there may be a far more innocent explanation for Da Vinci's final masterpiece. However, like I've repeatedly written throughout this book, it's just speculation from an open mind.

Conclusion

I would like to conclude by just saying that we simply cannot know anything for certain. I personally would like to believe that there is more to Jesus' story than what we think we know from the Biblical and Gnostic sources but I'm not going to make a statement that is bold without concrete evidence. I have tried throughout the book to put forward interesting pieces of evidence without intervening too much with imposing opinions. This is so that you can make your own mind up about what is truth and what is just nonsense.

I'd like to take this opportunity to thank you for reading this book and I do hope you enjoyed it. Even if you think there is an element of lunacy to my theories, it is my wish that you had a bit of fun along the way. We cannot know nor say for certain whether Jesus was an extraterrestrial or not. Nor can we determine one way or another whether or not he was sent here by extraterrestrials who visited us in a distant past. But we might one day…and if such a day arrives, I hope I look a little less crazy if the evidence points in favour of the statements I made in this book. I truly believe that there are a lot of mysteries in the ancient world that do point to the existence of advanced beings who came to our planet long ago. If we're able to find indisputable evidence of such interactions with our species and if it turns out there are more shards of Jesus' story that come to light which favour this narrative, the implications would be revolutionary for our species and our understanding of where we came from.

Bibliography

1. Aslan, Reza, *Zealot: The Life and Times of Jesus of Nazareth*, (The Westbourne Press, 2014).

2. Meyer, Marvin, *The Nag Hammadi Scriptures: The Revised and Updated Translation of Sacred Gnostic Texts Complete in One Volume*, (HarperOne International, 2009).

3. Rael, Claude, *The Final Message: Humanity's Origins and Our Future Explained*, (Tagman Press, 1998).

4. Von Daniken, Erich, *Chariots of the Gods: Was God an Astronaut?*, (Souvenir Press Ltd, 1990).

5. Von Daniken, Erich, *History is Wrong*, (New Page Books, 2009).

6. Von Daniken, Erich, *The Gods Never Left Us*, (New Page Books, 2017).

7. The Holy Bible, *New International Version*, (Collins, 2011).

More by Adrienne Jaffery…

TheOuterWorldBooks

Copyright 2020

Printed in Poland
by Amazon Fulfillment
Poland Sp. z o.o., Wrocław

58773769R00082